1. Introduction

The financial crisis had its roots in, as well as profound effects on, housing and mortgage markets, affecting many households, lenders, investors, and the overall health of the economy. The large declines in house prices eroded households' housing equity and left many borrowers underwater and at risk of default (Mayer et al. (2009)). The resulting wave of defaults left lenders and investors on the hook for losses that depleted (and sometimes exhausted) funds available to cover those losses. And the resulting collapse of building activity and the financial markets led to a severe recession with a dramatic rise in the unemployment rate.

The Federal Reserve quickly stepped in, pushing the fed funds rate toward zero and embarking on a path of extraordinarily accommodative policy, in which the Fed committed to purchasing Treasury securities and mortgage-backed securities (MBS) with the stated goal of supporting the housing market by lowering mortgage rates. The resulting boost to the housing market was expected to help bring a halt to, and then hopefully begin to reverse the slide in house prices, increase household wealth, and spur household consumption. Several papers have examined the effects of Federal Reserve large-scale asset purchase programs on longer-term interest rates. Hancock and Passmore (2014) show that Federal Reserve purchases lowered mortgage rates, while Stroebel and Taylor (2012) show that these purchases had little effect on mortgage rates. Fuster and Willen (2010) and Fuster et al. (2014), using data on the menu of mortgage rates and points available to borrowers, found substantial effects of the Federal Reserve's asset purchase programs on MBS yields and mortgage rates.

But even if the Federal Reserve was successful in lowering longer-term interest rates and therefore mortgage rates, the effects on mortgage borrowers may be less clear-cut. The reduction in MBS yields due to Federal Reserve MBS purchases were not entirely passed through in the form of lower mortgage rates. Scharfstein and Sunderam (2014) cite the lack of a competitive market structure as the primary

1

obstacle to transmitting these savings through to mortgage borrowers. Fuster, et al. (2012) attribute the lack of pass-through in part to fatter profit margins earned by originators, as well as higher costs. Many industry participants cited higher guarantee fees charged by the housing GSEs, but also cited lender capacity constraints, driven by the unanticipated bulge in refinancing demand that strained the processing capacity that remained after the 2008-2009 mortgage industry contraction.

Our study provides a complementary analysis which focuses on the quantity of mortgage originations, and how the interplay of refinancing demand and industry processing capacity affected the type of borrower able to access the market. We show that the spread between mortgage rates faced by new mortgage borrowers and the yield on agency MBS is positively correlated with the extent to which mortgage originators were capacity constrained in producing additional mortgages. Moreover, we show that lenders showed no visible propensity to expand capacity in response to increased refinance volumes. Rather, lenders expand and contract their mortgage staffs as the volume of purchase mortgage demand expands and contracts through a slow process. This pattern is of behavior is plausible when refinancing waves are expected to be relatively short-lived.

When lenders are capacity constrained, they might have the ability to choose which mortgage applications to complete and originate. We show, both theoretically and empirically, that capacity-constrained lenders are likely to bias their selection away from applicants of relatively higher credit risk toward those of lower credit risk, whose mortgages are generally easier and thus less costly to complete. As capacity constraints ease, lenders then turn to underwriting the riskier and more-difficult-to-complete mortgage applications. We show that, as a result, it is entirely possible that purchase originations among relatively higher credit-risk borrowers increase (or at least don't fall as quickly as originations among lower credit-risk borrowers) following a rise in interest rates, as the effect of relaxed capacity constraint at least partially offsets the higher cost of mortgage credit on their demand for loans. This contrasts with the more normal negative response of mortgage originations among lower credit-risk borrowers to higher interest rates.

Indeed, our estimates suggest that a decrease in capacity utilization consistent with that seen from early 2013 to late 2013 could increase purchase originations by 20-30 percent among borrowers with low credit scores (620 or less), 20-25 percent among borrowers with credit scores of 621-680, 8-14 percent among borrowers with credit scores of 681-710, and up to 8 percent among borrowers with credit scores of 711-740. In some cases, the boost coming from lower capacity utilization more than offsets the drag caused by higher mortgage rates.

The remainder of this paper is organized as follows. Section 2 provides some background and some key empirical facts that guided our thinking and estimation and summarizes the data we use. Section 3 presents our theoretical model and Section 4 discusses our empirical strategy and results. Section 5 concludes.

2. Data and Stylized Facts

The housing market saw a sea change along many dimensions following the onset of the financial crisis. Amidst the steep decline in housing prices, soaring delinquencies and mortgage defaults, the collapse of prominent mortgage lenders, and the conservatorship of Fannie Mae and Freddie Mac, the number of purchase originations plunged to about half their previously prevailing levels (see Avery et al. (2010a, 2010b)). This can be seen in Figure 1A, which shows monthly purchase applications and originations from the Home Mortgage Disclosure Act (HMDA) data during 2003-2014.[2,3] Refinance

activity, however, held up fairly well, propped up by historically low mortgage rates (Figure 1B).

But the decline in purchase originations does not reveal the fundamental character of the

underlying change. Similar to the findings in Bhutta (2014), the pullback in credit supply (and demand,

for that matter) has been very different among borrowers with different credit-risk profiles. We

therefore augment the HMDA data with the monthly *proportion* of originations that fall within various

credit-score ranges by mortgage product type[4] based on the proportions observed in the LPS / Black

Knight data. In particular, we define seven credit-score groups among the prime GSE mortgages

contained within the LPS / Black Knight data: 620 or less, 621-680, 681-710, 711-740, 741-770, 771-790,

and greater than 790. In the end, the combined data allow us to approximate monthly purchase and

refinance originations among each of these credit-score groups during 2003-2014.

These data are plotted in Figure 2. Purchase originations to borrowers with near-average (prime)

credit scores, those with scores in the 710-740 range, have been cut to less than half their mid-2000s

pace. The number of loans to borrowers with lower credit scores (620-680) has shrunk to around 10

percent of their mid-2000s pace. At the same time, among borrowers with very high credit scores, the

"super-prime" group (with scores exceeding 790), the pace of purchase originations did not really step

down post-crisis. As a result, as shown in Figure 3, the 10th-percentile credit scores on new purchase

originations and new refinance originations moved up sharply during the financial crisis, as lenders and

---

[2] As the HMDA data are currently available only through the end of 2013, we use data from the Mortgage Bankers Association's Weekly Applications Survey to estimate the total number of HMDA applications for October 2013 – September 2014 and the total number of HMDA originations for January 2014 – September 2014. The regression results are contained in Table A.1 in the Appendix.

[3] The HMDA data cover 80-90 percent of the mortgage market and are described in detail in Bhutta and Ringo (2014) among many others.

[4] We partition the LPS / Black Knight data into Fannie Mae / Freddie Mac (GSE), FHA/VA, private-label securitized (jumbo, alt-A, and subprime mortgages), and bank portfolio loans and adjust for differential data coverage of these market segments.

homeowners alike reevaluated their tolerance for credit risk. Therefore, in our empirical work to follow, we exclude the crisis period itself, and model the behavior of mortgage originations post-crises period separately from the pre-crises period, spans of time during which credit-score distributions were relatively stable: January 2003 to June 2007 and July 2009 to September 2014.

In the aftermath of the financial crisis, mortgage lenders cut their mortgage staffs dramatically. In particular, according to data from the Bureau of Labor and Statistics, the total number of employees working in the mortgage industry in the U.S. peaked at about 500,000 around the end of 2005.[5] By the end of 2008, total industry staffing had been cut nearly in half (Figure 4A). While mortgage industry employment and purchase mortgage activity both plunged during the financial crisis, the pace of refinancing activity rebounded to pre-crisis levels in the first half of 2009 and for again for much of the period from late 2010-2013 amidst large and persistent declines in mortgage interest rates. Indeed, the pace of refinancing activity during much of the latter period was enough to cause lenders to cite capacity constraints as a major hurdle to passing through interest rate savings onto borrowers (Fuster et al. 2012).

To gauge how the dramatic changes in industry employment might have strained mortgage industry capacity, we construct a measure of capacity utilization based on a simple productivity concept: mortgage demand per industry employee. The broadest measure one might consider would be equal to total mortgage applications in a given month divided by the number of industry employees available that month. We focus on a somewhat narrower measure, based solely on the number of refinancing applications, which will have the benefit of being somewhat exogenous, or at least distinct, from our

---

[5] The real estate credit and mortgage and non-mortgage loan broker employment components we use from BLS likely overstate the number of employees who solely process mortgage applications.

main empirical measure of mortgage demand, purchase applications.[6] To account for lags in processing

and completing applications when capacity utilization is high, we use a (geometrically) weighted average

of refinance applications over the past four months, divided by the number of mortgage-related

employees available to process and complete those applications that month. Our capacity utilization

measure is shown in Figure 4B. Clearly, capacity utilization during much of the period between 2009

thru the first half of 2013 ran well above the level that prevailed during most of the pre-crisis period.

If capacity constraints effectively convey temporary market power to mortgage lenders, then this

should affect both pricing and quantities, compared to a world where supply was highly elastic. Figure

4B shows our measure of capacity utilization plotted alongside a price measure of capacity constraint:

the interest rate spread between the 30-year fixed-rate mortgage rate and the 30-year current-coupon

mortgage-backed security (MBS) yield. As shown in Fuster et al. (2012) and Scharfstein and Sunderam

(2014), this spread tends to increase when mortgage capacity is strained: Lenders have an incentive to

(jointly and individually) control the flow of arriving refinance applications by not decreasing mortgage

rates in line with MBS yields.[7,8]

Gauging the effect on quantities, the subject of our study, is a bit more subtle. We argue, in

particular, that an important quantity effect was to skew underwriting resources away from borrowers

requiring more effort, generally those without pristine credit records or easily documented regular

---

[6] Because the number of mortgages for refinancing is generally much larger than the number of purchase
mortgages, particularly since 2009, excluding purchase applications from the numerator does not have a very large
effect on our capacity utilization measure, that is, measures that include and exclude purchase applications are
quite highly correlated.

[7] Lenders might also exercise a form of price discrimination by charging relatively high mortgage rates to
borrowers who have the largest incentives to refinance, before lowering mortgage rates to entice additional
borrowers, with smaller incentives, to refinance.

[8] In addition, the nature of future commitments and the secondary TBA market provide disincentives for lenders
and secondary-market participants to move rates down too quickly: Lenders have committed to deliver a certain
volume of mortgages with pre-specified characteristics to the secondary market, while secondary market
participants have committed to deliver TBA pools of mortgages with pre-specified characteristics.

income. Before moving on to the modeling, one suggestive piece of evidence of this effect is provided in Figure 5, which plots our main capacity utilization measure alongside the 10th-percentile credit score among new purchase and refinance originations over the post-crisis period. As shown, when capacity utilization tends to be high, the 10th-percentile credit score among borrowers getting mortgages also tends to be relatively high.

We use several other sources for auxiliary data. In particular, we use the monthly national unemployment rate from the Bureau of Labor Statistics, and compute monthly data on year-over-year house price growth from CoreLogic data, monthly average mortgage rates from Freddie Mac and LoanSifter / Optimal Blue data, and monthly average current-coupon MBS yields from Barclays data. Each of these data series is available during 2003-2014.

In the remainder of the paper, we attempt to examine the underlying relationship between capacity constraints and credit availability, and provide a model to help interpret it.

3. Model

We offer a fairly simple model of the mortgage originator's decision on the range of borrower credit risks and the number of purchase and refinance mortgage applications that it will process in a given period, assuming it faces an inelastic supply of underwriting resources, i.e., trained labor. The focus of this model is thus a somewhat interesting and presumably relevant example of how a producer might optimally allocate an inelastically supplied input to the production of multiple outputs. We then use this simple model to examine how changes in the demand for mortgages driven by market interest rates can affect the allocation of those underwriting resources.

The lender is assumed to be a price taker, with the revenue earned on each mortgage determined by the housing government-sponsored enterprises (GSEs) that purchase the mortgages. As shown in Table 1A, which shows a portion of a mortgage rate sheet for an anonymous lender, lenders offer a menu of mortgage rates and up-front points to be paid by the borrower when the mortgage closes. Historically, the trade-off between mortgage rates and up-front points is around one-sixth of a percentage point on the mortgage rate per up-front point. So a borrower wishing to pay no up-front points might receive a mortgage rate of 3.50 or 3.625, while a comparable borrower willing to pay around two up-front points would receive a mortgage rate of 3.25.

The lender would then sell these two mortgages into the TBA market. The net proceeds for each mortgage would depend on the TBA price (the price paid by the GSEs to acquire a mortgage meeting the TBA guidelines), base servicing costs, guarantee fees, and any g-fee buydowns or excess servicing (see Fuster et al. (2012) for a more detailed description and an example). Moreover, as shown in Table 1B, lenders also face loan-level pricing adjustments in which the GSEs charge for perceived credit risk. For example, the lender would be required to pay 0.75 percentage points for extending a mortgage to a borrower with a 20-percent downpayment and a credit score of 720, and 2.75 percentage points for a similar borrower with a credit score of 660. In sum, the secondary mortgage market and the GSEs are the primary drivers of the pricing of a mortgage, irrespective of the mortgage note rate.[9]

Total demand, or applications received, for purchase mortgages, $a_n(i)$, and for refinance mortgages, $a_r(i)$ is assumed to depend negatively on the level of market interest rates. That is, borrowers submit fewer mortgage applications when interest rates are higher. Moreover, it is assumed

---

[9] While it is true that an investor in the secondary market will pay more for a higher-yielding security, mortgages tend to be bundled into MBS pools with a specified yield. But a lender delivering a mortgage with a high note rate will likely have to pay discount points to the borrower, while a lender delivering a mortgage with a low note rate will likely receive points from the borrower.

that the refinance mortgage demand is more sensitive to interest rates than demand for purchase

mortgages; in particular, $a_r' < a_n' < 0$.

The most important assumption underlying our analysis is that the labor resource cost for

underwriting either a purchase (or refinance) mortgage u_n (u_r) is increasing in the borrower's credit

risk, as measured, for instance, by their credit history. The underwriting cost of a purchase (or "new")

mortgage, for any given borrower credit risk, is assumed to be higher than the cost of a refinance

mortgage, by a factor of $\theta > 1$, though this is less critical to the analysis. In order to keep the analytics

simple, and without loss of generality, we assume that the range of borrower underwriting costs for a

refinance mortgage is measured on the unit interval [0, 1]. Thus, refinance (and purchase) applications

at the top of the credit-risk spectrum, the most costly to underwrite, cost 1 unit of labor ($u = 1$),

whereas the least costly refinance mortgages to underwrite, those with the lowest credit risk, cost no

resources ($u = 0$). Similarly, the range of borrower underwriting costs for a purchase mortgage is

measured on the interval [0, θ], with θ denoting the cost of the most costly, highest credit-risk purchase

mortgage. As shown in the Appendix, our results are robust to the more general and plausible

assumption of a strictly positive but relatively small marginal cost for underwriting the lowest credit-risk

borrowers.

The lender's problem is thus to choose credit-risk "cut-off" levels, i.e., the highest credit-risk

purchase and refinance applications, having per-unit costs, u_n and u_r, respectively, that it is willing to

underwrite. The lender processes and completes all the applications it receives with costs at or below

those cutoff levels. The terms u_n and u_r thus represent the proportion of purchase and refinance

applications processed and completed: The total quantity of mortgages originated (i.e., the number of

applications processed and completed) is $\int_0^{u_n} a_n \, du + \int_0^{u_r} a_r \, du = u_n a_n + u_r a_r$. Note that this implies that the credit risk of arriving applications is assumed to be uniformly distributed. Moreover, the range and distribution of application borrower credit risk is independent of interest rates.

Assuming that the lender faces a wage rate per unit of underwriting labor equal to $w > 0$, then the cost of processing and completing mortgage applications is $w\theta \int_0^{u_n} u a_n \, du + w \int_0^{u_r} u a_r \, du$. In addition, we assume that the lender faces a labor capacity constraint which can limit the number of mortgages it can originate: $\theta \int_0^{u_n} u a_n \, du + \int_0^{u_r} u a_r \, du \leq L$, where L is the amount of labor the lender has available. Note that, while we use an explicit constraint, analogous results can be shown in a model where the firm faces a labor cost function that is convex in the quantity of labor used.

The lender's profit function therefore takes the form

$$p u_n a_n + p u_r a_r - w\theta \int_0^{u_n} u a_n \, du - w \int_0^{u_r} u a_r \, du,$$

which it maximizes with respect to its choice of u_n and u_r, subject to the capacity constraint

$$\theta \int_0^{u_n} u a_n \, du + \int_0^{u_r} u a_r \, du \leq L.$$

This leads to the following three propositions, the first of which relates the cut-off underwriting cost (borrower credit risk) for purchase originations to that for refinance originations (all proofs are given in the Appendix).

Proposition 1. *Lenders will be more inclined to extend higher up the credit-risk spectrum for refinance borrowers than for purchase borrowers. That is, $u_r > u_n$.*

In essence, lenders are indifferent between processing and completing a purchase application with underwriting cost u^* and a refinance application with underwriting cost θu^*. The next proposition compares the interest-rate sensitivity of the cut-off underwriting costs for purchase and refinance originations.

Proposition 2. *When lenders are capacity constrained, a rise in interest rates will result in lenders extending their range of lending to higher credit-risk purchase and refinance borrowers. Furthermore, their increased willingness to lend to higher credit-risk borrowers as a result of the rise will be larger for refinance borrowers. That is, $\frac{\partial u_r}{\partial i} > \frac{\partial u_n}{\partial i} > 0$.*

In other words, the cut-off credit risk (the highest credit-risk borrower with access to a loan) drops as interest rates rise and total demand for loans falls. Moreover, the cut-off underwriting cost for refinance originations is more interest-rate sensitive than for purchase originations. The final proposition provides conditions under which purchase originations can increase when interest rates rise.

Proposition 3. *When lenders are capacity constrained, a rise in interest rates will result in a decline in total lending to refinance borrowers; on the contrary, a rise in interest rates will, under some conditions, result in a rise in total lending to purchase borrowers. That is, $\frac{\partial u_r a_r}{\partial i} < 0$ always holds but under some conditions $\frac{\partial u_n a_n}{\partial i} > 0$. Necessary (but not sufficient) conditions under which a rise in interest rates boosts total purchase lending include:*

- $\varepsilon_n \, / \, \varepsilon_r \ll 1$ *(where ε_n and ε_r denote the interest rate elasticities of purchase and refinance applications, respectively), i.e., refinance applications are far more interest rate elastic than purchase applications.*

- $\theta \gg 1$*, i.e., purchase applications are more expensive to process and complete than refinance applications.*

- $a_n \, / \, a_r \ll 1$*, i.e., the number of purchase applications is substantially lower than number of refinance applications.*

That is, the positive effect of the easing of capacity constraints can at least partially offset the negative effect of higher interest rates under certain, fairly plausible, conditions. For example, one set of reasonably plausible parameters under which rising interest rates will induce an increase in purchase originations is when (i) the interest rate elasticity of refinance applications is 3 times the interest rate elasticity of purchase applications, (ii) there are twice as many refinance applications as purchase applications, and (iii) the relative cost of underwriting a purchase mortgage is the same or greater than that of underwriting a refinance mortgage of similar credit risk. Such conditions seem quite likely to hold, for instance, when interest rates are near historically low levels.

In the empirical work to follow, we test the implications of these three propositions. First, we will show that lenders are more willing to extend credit to higher credit-risk refinance borrowers than higher credit-risk purchase borrowers (Proposition 1). Second, we will show that credit risk is positively related to interest rates for both refinance and purchase originations and that the credit risk of refinance originations is more sensitive than purchase originations to interest rates (Proposition 2). Third, we will show that it is indeed possible to observe increased purchase originations when interest rates rise, as the positive effect of easing capacity constraints can at least partially offset the negative effect of higher interest rates (Proposition 3).

4. Estimation and Results

Mortgage Employees

The first thing we examine are the short-run dynamics of mortgage-related employees, that is, the sensitivity of aggregate industry employees to purchase and refinancing applications. Capacity constraints on making purchase mortgages that result from a steep rise in refinancing activity are not inevitable, but would occur only if hiring was not very responsive to swings in refinancing activity. One might not expect much sensitivity to refinancing activity if lenders view refinancing waves as being relatively short-lived reactions to temporarily low interest rates. Even in the presence of low but stable interest rates, refinancing waves wane due to borrower "burn-out" and the presence of borrowers who do not refinance when they have the incentive to do so (Schwartz and Torous (1989), Deng and Quigley (2006), and Campbell (2006)). To briefly examine the relative importance of purchase versus refinancing activity on industry employment, we consider the following regression:

$$\log(L)_t = \beta_0 + \sum_{k=1}^{12} \beta_{1k} \log(a_n)_{t-k} + \sum_{k=1}^{12} \beta_{1k} \log(a_r)_{t-k}.$$

The regression results are shown in Table 2. As can be seen, total mortgage staffing is strongly correlated with purchase applications. Lenders seemingly adjust only slowly, if at all, to refinance applications. So when interest rates decline and the demand for refinancing picks up, it appears that lenders behave as if they are "stuck" with their level of mortgage staffing, causing capacity utilization to increase. This is consistent with Fuster and Willen (2010), who find evidence that lenders were caught off-guard by the surge in refinance applications. We provide evidence below that when capacity utilization is elevated, lenders appear to favor originating relatively lower credit-risk, less-costly-to-produce mortgages, to the apparent detriment of borrowers with relatively high credit risk.

Credit Scores

Given our presumption that applications from borrowers with higher credit risk tend to involve greater underwriting costs, particularly in the post-crisis era, we estimate the relationship between the distribution of credit scores on new prime GSE originations and capacity utilization in the previous month. In particular, we use the 10th-percentile credit score among purchase originations as a (inverse) proxy for u_n, the high end of the underwriting cost range among purchase applications processed by the originator. The lower is the 10th-percentile credit score, the larger is the range of underwriting cost (u_n) that the originator covers. We thus consider regressions of the form

$$(1 - u)_t = \beta_0 + \beta_1 \left(\frac{a_r}{L}\right)_{t-1} + \beta_3 X_{t-1} + v_{it},$$

where $(1 - u)_t$ denotes the 10th-percentile credit scores on new purchase originations or refinance originations in month t, $\left(\frac{a_r}{L}\right)_{t-1}$ is capacity utilization in month $t - 1$, and X_{t-1} is a vector of controls, such as the year-over-year change in house prices, the year-over-year change in mortgage rates, the unemployment rate, and a time trend.[10] Table 3 shows the regression results, which reveal several important facts. First, higher credit scores are associated with higher capacity utilization for both purchase originations and refinance originations. This result is consistent with the prediction of Proposition 2, in which we hypothesized that $\frac{\partial u_n}{\partial i} > 0$ and $\frac{\partial u_r}{\partial i} > 0$. Furthermore, the final column shows the results when the difference between monthly credit scores on purchase originations versus refinance originations is used as the dependent variable. Here, the estimated constant is positive and statistically significant, indicating that $u_r > u_n$, which is consistent with the prediction of Proposition 1. Moreover, credit scores on refinance originations are more sensitive to our capacity utilization measure, so that $\frac{\partial u_r}{\partial i} > \frac{\partial u_n}{\partial i} > 0$, which is consistent with the penultimate prediction of Proposition 2.

All else being equal, these results suggest that an increase in capacity utilization of 4 applications per employee (a move consistent with that seen from early 2011 to mid 2012) increases the 10th-percentile credit score on new purchase originations by about 6 points. Similarly, the increase in capacity utilization increases the 10th-percentile credit score on new refinance originations by about 16 points. This provides evidence that higher credit-risk applicants appear to be adversely affected by high capacity

---

[10] We de-mean the independent variables in these regressions to in order to interpret the constant as the mean value of the 10th-percentile credit score over each period.

utilization. Indeed, as capacity utilization declined during the latter half of 2013, credit scores on newly originated mortgages declined. It bears noting, however, that these effects pale in comparison to the drastic pull-back in lending that followed the financial crisis, when 10th-percentile credit scores jumped 60-80 points, likely as a result of lenders and homeowners reevaluating their tolerance for risk.

Purchase Mortgage Originations

Our model from Section 3 also implies that not only the distribution, but also the number of mortgage originations will be sensitive to the cost of underwriting, which varies with credit risk and mortgage type. To more directly examine the differential effect of capacity constraints on originations for borrowers of varying credit risk, we estimate separate regressions for new purchase originations falling into seven credit-score buckets: 620 or less, 621-680, 681-710, 711-740, 741-770, 771-790, and greater than 790.

Throughout our analysis, we use total purchase applications to proxy for the underlying demand for purchase mortgages. As shown in Figure 6, data obtained from Optimal Blue on locked mortgage applications during 2013-2014 suggest that, at least in recent years, purchase applications from different credit-score groups tended to move together quite closely, except for the very lowest credit-score group (perhaps because of still relatively tight mortgage credit conditions). Because we estimate separate regressions for each credit-score group, the effect of total purchase applications on purchase originations are allowed to vary across credit-score groups. Finally, we expect high capacity utilization to act as a drag on originations, particularly for higher credit-risk, more-costly-to-complete mortgage originations; that is, when capacity utilization is higher, purchase applications do not translate into as many originations. This could be due to higher denial rates or longer origination timelines.

Our baseline empirical model takes the form

$$\log(u_n a_n)_{it} = \beta_0 + \beta_1 \left(\frac{a_r}{L}\right)_{t-1} + \beta_2 \log(a_n)_{t-1} + \beta_3 X_{t-1} + v_{it},$$

where $(u_n a_n)_{it}$ is the number of new prime GSE purchase originations for credit-score group i during

month t, $\left(\frac{a_r}{L}\right)_{t-1}$ is capacity utilization in month $t-1$, $(a_n)_{t-1}$ is the number of purchase applications,

and X_{t-1} is a vector of controls, such as the unemployment rate and a time trend. The prediction of

Proposition 3 is that $\beta_1 < 0$, particularly among borrowers in the lower credit-score groups.

Table 4 contains our parameter estimates for prime GSE purchase originations for the post-crisis

period (July 2009 to September 2014) in the upper panel, and the pre-crisis period (January 2003 to June

2007) in the lower panel. First, these results reveal that purchase originations for each credit-score

group are positively related to lagged aggregate purchase applications, $\log(a_n)_{t-1}$.[11] Second, and

consistent with the prediction of Proposition 3, higher capacity utilization tends to hold back purchase

originations among the low to middle credit-score groups (620 or lower, 621-680, and 681-710), while

lower capacity utilization tends to support purchase originations for these credit-score groups. This

implies that any easing of capacity utilization could at least partially offset the standard interest-rate

effect.

Note that in the pre-crisis period our capacity utilization measure enters the estimation results with

the expected sign and is statistically significant only for the 621-680 credit-score group. We would argue

that the lack of negative capacity utilization effects during the pre-crises period would be consistent

with the view that the cost of underwriting higher credit-risk borrowers was substantially lower prior to

the financial crisis. For example, Fuster et al. (2012) show several indicators of lower costs, including

---

[11] This relationship can break down if, for instance, lending to lower credit score borrowers became unhinged from
the overall volume of purchase applications, as underwriters might have focused more on expected house prices.

lower guarantee fees charged by the GSEs and shorter origination timelines, while Mayer et al. (2009) and Demyanyk and van Hemert (2011) point to less-scrupulous underwriting standards.

All else equal, these results suggest that a decrease in capacity utilization of about 4 applications per employee (a move consistent with that seen from 2012 to 2013) would result in over 30 percent more purchase originations among the lowest credit-score group (620 or less), 25 percent more for the 621-680 credit-score group, and 12 percent more for the 681-710 credit-score group. This effect would at least partially offset lower application volumes resulting from higher mortgage rates. Thus, it would appear that higher credit-risk applicants may have been adversely affected by the extraordinarily low interest rates, which helped to drive the elevated pace of refinancing by very low credit-risk borrowers, and thus, the elevated level of capacity utilization in the post-crisis period.

Next, we consider a simple nonlinear variant of our capacity utilization variable. In particular, we assume that capacity utilization only matters when it is above average: the capacity utilization variable is thus measured as the maximum of zero and the gap between capacity utilization and its average level. This specification takes the form

$$(1-u)_t = \beta_0 + \beta_1 \max\left\{\left(\frac{a_r}{L}\right)_{t-1} - \frac{\overline{a_r}}{L}, 0\right\} + \beta_3 X_{t-1} + v_{it}$$

for credit scores on new mortgage originations and

$$\log(u_n a_n)_{it} = \beta_0 + \beta_1 \max\left\{\left(\frac{a_r}{L}\right)_{t-1} - \frac{\overline{a_r}}{L}, 0\right\} + \beta_2 \log(a_n)_{t-1} + \beta_3 X_{t-1} + v_{it}$$

for the number of new purchase originations, where $\frac{\overline{a_r}}{L}$ denotes mean capacity utilization during 2003-2014.[12] The results (presented in Table 5 for credit scores and Table 6 for purchase originations) are similar to those of our primary specification. The coefficients on capacity utilization are often somewhat larger in the nonlinear version, while the regression fit (R-squared) is sometimes slightly higher and other times a bit lower. Consistent with the predictions of Propositions 1-3, higher credit scores are associated with greater capacity utilization for both purchase and refinance originations, credit scores on refinance originations are more sensitive to capacity utilization, and higher capacity utilization tends to hold back purchase originations among the low to middle credit-score groups (620 or lower, 621-680, 681-710, and 711-740).

These results suggest that, all else equal, a decrease in above-average capacity utilization of about 2 applications per employee (a move consistent with that seen from 2012 to 2013) could result in an increased 10th-percentile credit score on new purchase originations of about 3 points, an increased 10th-percentile credit score on new refinance originations of about 12 points. Our regression using the number of purchase originations suggests that the effect would be to increase purchase originations by about 33 percent, 27 percent, 14 percent, and 8 percent for the 620 or less, 621-680, 681-710, and 711-740 credit-score groups, respectively.

Robustness Tests

Our first robustness check alters our primary specification by using the interest rate spread between the 30-year fixed-rate mortgage rate and the 30-year current-coupon MBS yield as an alternative, price-

---

[12] The maximum function shown here is equivalent to an indicator function for above-average capacity utilization interacted with the gap between capacity utilization and its average level: $\mathbb{I}\left\{\left(\frac{a_r}{L}\right)_{t-1} \geq \frac{\overline{a_r}}{L}\right\}\left[\left(\frac{a_r}{L}\right)_{t-1} - \frac{\overline{a_r}}{L}\right]$, where $\mathbb{I}\{\cdot\}$ denotes the indicator function taking on the value one when $\left(\frac{a_r}{L}\right)_{t-1} \geq \frac{\overline{a_r}}{L}$ and zero otherwise. We use the simpler, "maximum" notation throughout.

based measure of capacity utilization. This spread tends to increase when mortgage capacity is strained, as lenders have an incentive to (jointly and individually) reduce the supply of refinancing by not decreasing mortgage rates in line with MBS yields or by exercising some degree of price discrimination. In addition, their mortgage pricing may be bound by institutional frictions in the mortgage market (see, for example, Fuster et al. (2012) and Scharfstein and Sunderam (2014)). This alternative specification takes the form

$$(1 - u)_t = \beta_0 + \beta_1 (frm - mbs)_{t-1} + \beta_3 X_{t-1} + v_{it}$$

for credit scores on new mortgage originations and

$$\log(u_n a_n)_{it} = \beta_0 + \beta_1 (frm - mbs)_{t-1} + \beta_2 \log(a_n)_{t-1} + \beta_3 X_{t-1} + v_{it},$$

for the number of new purchase originations, where $(frm - mbs)_{t-1}$ is the average interest rate spread (mortgage rate minus MBS yield spread) in month $t - 1$. The results (presented in Table 7 for credit scores and Table 8 for purchase originations) are similar to those of our primary specification. Higher credit scores are associated with greater capacity utilization for both purchase and refinance originations; credit scores on refinance originations are more sensitive than purchase originations to capacity utilization; and higher capacity utilization tends to hold back purchase originations among lower credit-score groups (620 or less, 621-680, and 681-710).

These results suggest that, all else equal, a decline in the interest rate spread of about 40 basis points (a move consistent with that seen from 2012 to 2013) could result in an increased 10th-percentile credit score on new purchase originations of about 3 points, and an increased 10th-percentile credit score on new refinance originations of about 13 points, and increased purchase originations of about 21 percent, 21 percent, and 8 percent for the less than 620, 621-680, and 681-710 credit-score groups, respectively.

Our final two robustness checks alter our initial specification by (i) adding an additional lag for the number of purchase applications on the right-hand-side of our estimation equation so that

$$\log(u_n a_n)_{it} = \beta_0 + \beta_1 \left(\frac{a_r}{L}\right)_{t-1} + \beta_{21} \log(a_n)_{t-1} + \beta_{22} \log(a_n)_{t-2} + \beta_3 X_{t-1} + v_{it},$$

and (ii) placing the number of purchase applications on the left-hand-side of our estimation equation, so that the dependent variable is the log of the ratio of (credit-score group) originations to total purchase applications,

$$\log(u_n a_n)_{it} - \log(a_n)_{t-1} = \beta_0 + \beta_1 \left(\frac{a_r}{L}\right)_{t-1} + \beta_3 X_{t-1} + v_{it}.$$

These results are reported in Tables 9 and 10, respectively. As before, higher capacity utilization tends to hold back purchase originations among the lower credit-score groups (620 or less, 621-680, and 681-710).

In total, our results provide evidence that mortgage lenders, when constrained, produce lower credit-risk mortgages more readily than higher credit-risk mortgages. During the most recent mortgage refinance wave of 2011-2013, refinancing activity more than doubled, but lenders (eventually) increased their mortgage staffs by less than 20 percent. This left lenders capacity constrained and, as a result, we hypothesize that lenders had a preference to complete relatively lower credit-risk, less costly, and quicker-to-complete mortgages. As a result, we found that credit scores on new mortgage originations tended to increase during mortgage refinancing booms, when lenders had higher capacity utilization, and then tended to decrease afterward. Similarly, we found that higher credit-risk purchase originations were suppressed during recent mortgage refinancing waves, when lenders were most constrained, in favor of lower credit-risk purchase and refinance mortgages.

5. Conclusion

We present evidence suggesting that binding mortgage processing capacity constraints reduce mortgage originations to borrowers with low to modest credit scores. Mortgage processing capacity constraints typically bind when the demand for mortgage refinancing shifts outward, usually because of lower mortgage rates. As a result, high capacity utilization leads mortgage lenders to ration mortgage credit, completing mortgages that require less underwriting resources, and are thus less costly, to produce. This is hypothesized to have a particularly adverse impact on relatively higher credit-risk borrowers' ability to obtain mortgages. What is more, we show that, by lowering capacity utilization, a rise in interest rates can, under certain circumstances, induce an increase in mortgage originations to relatively higher risk borrowers. In particular, we find fairly large effects for purchasing borrowers with low to modest credit scores, in which we find that a decrease in capacity utilization of 4 applications per mortgage employee (similar to the moves observed from 2012 to 2013) could result in *increased* purchase mortgage originations, as the relaxed capacity constraint might have offset any negative effect on mortgage demand from higher interest rates.

Appendix

Proof of Proposition 1. Lenders maximize $p u_n a_n + p u_r a_r - w\theta \int_0^{u_n} u a_n\, du - w \int_0^{u_r} u a_r\, du$ with respect to u_n and u_r, subject to the capacity constraint $\theta \int_0^{u_n} u a_n\, du + \int_0^{u_r} u a_r\, du \leq L$. This leads to the following first-order conditions:

$$p - w\theta u_n - \lambda\theta u_n = 0$$

$$p - w u_r - \lambda u_r = 0$$

$$\lambda\left(\frac{1}{2}\theta u_n^2 a_n + \frac{1}{2}u_r^2 a_r - L\right) = 0,$$

where $\lambda \geq 0$ is the Lagrange multiplier on the capacity constraint. In the unconstrained case, $\lambda = 0$ so that $u_n = p/w\theta$ and $u_r = p/w$. Because $\theta > 1$, $u_r > u_n$. In the capacity constrained case, $\lambda > 0$. The first-order conditions yield $\lambda = \frac{p - w\theta u_n}{\theta u_n} = \frac{p - w u_r}{u_r}$ so that $u_r = \theta u_n$. Because $\theta > 1$, $u_r > u_n$. ∎

Proof of Proposition 2. When lenders are capacity constrained, $\theta u_n^2 a_n + u_r^2 a_r = 2L$. Further, $u_r = \theta u_n$ implies that $u_r^2 = \frac{2L\theta}{a_n + \theta a_r}$ and $u_n^2 = \frac{2L}{\theta(a_n + \theta a_r)}$. Differentiating and simplifying yields

$$\frac{\partial u_r}{\partial i} = \frac{1}{2u_r}\left[\frac{-2L\theta(a_n' + \theta a_r')}{(a_n + \theta a_r)^2}\right]$$

$$\frac{\partial u_n}{\partial i} = \frac{1}{2u_n}\left[\frac{-2L\theta(a_n' + \theta a_r')}{\theta^2(a_n + \theta a_r)^2}\right].$$

Because $u_r > 0$ and $u_n > 0$, it is sufficient to sign the numerators of these two expressions. Because $-2L\theta < 0$, $a_n' < 0$, and $a_r' < 0$, then $\frac{\partial u_r}{\partial i} > 0$ and $\frac{\partial u_n}{\partial i} > 0$. Further, because $u_r = \theta u_n$ and $\theta > 1$, $\frac{\partial u_r}{\partial i} = \theta\frac{\partial u_n}{\partial i} > 0$ so that $\frac{\partial u_r}{\partial i} > \frac{\partial u_n}{\partial i} > 0$. ∎

Proof of Proposition 3. $\frac{\partial u_r a_r}{\partial i} = \frac{1}{2(u_r a_r)}\frac{4L\theta(a_n + \theta a_r)a_r a_r' - 2L\theta a_r^2(a_n' + \theta a_r')}{(a_n + \theta a_r)^2}$. Because $u_r a_r > 0$, it is sufficient to sign the numerator of this expression, $4L\theta(a_n + \theta a_r)a_r a_r' - 2L\theta a_r^2(a_n' + \theta a_r') = 4L\theta a_n a_r a_r' + 2L\theta a_r^2(\theta a_r' - a_n')$. Because $\theta > 1$ and $a_r' < a_n' < 0$, $4L\theta a_n a_r a_r' + 2L\theta a_r^2(\theta a_r' - a_n') < 0$ so that $\frac{\partial u_r a_r}{\partial i} < 0$. $\frac{\partial u_n a_n}{\partial i} = \frac{1}{2(u_n a_n)}\frac{4L\theta(a_n + \theta a_r)a_n a_n' - 2L\theta a_n^2(a_n' + \theta a_r')}{\theta^2(a_n + \theta a_r)^2}$. Because $u_n a_n > 0$, it is sufficient to sign the numerator of this expression, $4L\theta(a_n + \theta a_r)a_n a_n' - 2L\theta a_n^2(a_n' + \theta a_r') = 2L\theta a_n^2 a_n' + 4L\theta^2 a_n a_r a_n' - 2L\theta^2 a_n^2 a_r'$. Under what conditions is this positive? $2L\theta a_n^2 a_n' + 4L\theta^2 a_n a_r a_n' - 2L\theta^2 a_n^2 a_r' > 0$ when $a_n a_n' + 2\theta a_r a_n' > \theta a_n a_r'$, which is equivalent to the condition that $\frac{(a_n + 2\theta a_r)a_n'}{\theta a_n a_r'} =$

22

$\left(\frac{1}{\theta} + 2\frac{a_r}{a_n}\right)\frac{a'_n}{a'_r} < 1$. Multiplying and dividing by $\frac{a_r}{a_n}$ yields $\left(\frac{1}{\theta}\frac{a_n}{a_r} + 2\right)\frac{\varepsilon_n}{\varepsilon_r} < 1$. For this latter inequality to

hold, $\varepsilon_n / \varepsilon_r \ll 1, \theta \gg 1$, and/or $a_n / a_r \ll 1$. ∎

Generalized Model. Here we generalize our model of the lender's decision on the credit risk of

mortgages it chooses to underwrite. To generalize, we relax the assumption that the least costly to

underwrite mortgage costs no resources ($u = 0$). We therefore assume that the range of borrower

underwriting costs for a refinance application is measured on the unit interval $[c, c + 1]$. Thus,

refinance applications at the bottom of the credit-risk spectrum, the least costly to underwrite, cost c,

whereas the most costly refinance mortgages to underwrite, those with the highest credit risk, cost $c +$

1. Similarly, underwriting costs for purchase applications range from θc for the lowest credit-risk

mortgages to $\theta(c + 1)$ for the highest credit-risk mortgages ($\theta > 1$).

As before, the lender takes prices as given and faces an exogenous flow of purchase and refinance

applications with $a'_r < a'_n < 0$. The lender then chooses credit-risk "cut off" levels, the highest credit-

risk purchase and refinance applications, having per-unit costs , u_n and u_r, that it is willing to incur in

underwriting purchase and refinance mortgages, respectively. The lender processes and completes all

the applications it receives with costs at or below those cutoff levels. The terms $u_n - c$ and $u_r - c$ thus

represent the proportion of purchase and refinance applications processed and completed: the total

quantity of mortgages originated (i.e., the number of mortgage applications processed and completed)

is $\int_c^{u_n} a_n \, du + \int_c^{u_r} a_r \, du = (u_n - c)a_n + (u_r - c)a_r$. Note that the credit-risk distribution of arriving

applications is uniformly distributed. Moreover, the range and distribution of application borrower

credit risk is independent of interest rates.

The lender still faces the separable cost function $w\theta \int_c^{u_n} ua_n \, du + w \int_c^{u_r} ua_r \, du$ in processing and

completing mortgage applications, as well as a labor capacity constraint which can limit the number of

mortgages it can originate: $\theta \int_c^{u_n} ua_n \, du + \int_c^{u_r} ua_r \, du \leq L$. This labor capacity constraint still acts as

the main mechanism by which lenders will crowd out high-cost purchase applications in favor of lower

cost purchase and refinance applications.

The lender's profit function therefore takes the form

$$p(u_n - c)a_n + p(u_r - c)a_r - w\theta \int_c^{u_n} ua_n \, du - w \int_c^{u_r} ua_r \, du,$$

which it maximizes with respect to its choice of u_n and u_r, subject to the capacity constraint

$$\theta \int_c^{u_n} u a_n \, du + \int_c^{u_r} u a_r \, du \leq L.$$

This leads to the following three propositions.

Proposition 1. *Lenders will be more inclined to extend higher up the credit-risk spectrum for refinance borrowers than for purchase borrowers. That is, $u_r > u_n$.*

Proof. The lender maximizes $p(u_n - c)a_n + p(u_r - c)a_r - w\theta \int_c^{u_n} u a_n \, du - w \int_c^{u_r} u a_r \, du$ with respect to u_n and u_r, subject to the capacity constraint $\theta \int_c^{u_n} u a_n \, du + \int_c^{u_r} u a_r \, du \leq L$. This leads to the following first-order conditions:

$$p - w\theta u_n - \lambda \theta u_n = 0$$

$$p - w u_r - \lambda u_r = 0$$

$$\lambda \left[\frac{1}{2}\theta(u_n^2 - c^2)a_n + \frac{1}{2}(u_r^2 - c^2)a_r - L \right] = 0,$$

where $\lambda \geq 0$ is the Lagrange multiplier on the capacity constraint. In the unconstrained case, $\lambda = 0$ so that $u_n = p/w\theta$ and $u_r = p/w$. Because $\theta > 1$, $u_r > u_n$. In the capacity constrained case, $\lambda > 0$. The first-order conditions yield $\lambda = \frac{p - w\theta u_n}{\theta u_n} = \frac{p - w u_r}{u_r}$ so that $u_r = \theta u_n$. Because $\theta > 1$, $u_r > u_n$. ∎

Proposition 2. *When lenders are capacity constrained, they will lend to higher credit-risk borrowers when interest rates rise. Furthermore, lenders' willingness to lend to higher credit-risk borrowers when interest rates rise will be greater for refinance borrowers. That is, $\frac{\partial u_r}{\partial i} > \frac{\partial u_n}{\partial i} > 0$.*

Proof. When lenders are capacity constrained, $\frac{1}{2}\theta(u_n^2 - c^2)a_n + \frac{1}{2}(u_r^2 - c^2)a_r = L$. Further, $u_r = \theta u_n$ implies that $u_r^2 = \frac{2L\theta + c^2\theta(\theta a_n + a_r)}{a_n + \theta a_r}$ and $u_n^2 = \frac{2L + c^2(\theta a_n + a_r)}{\theta(a_n + \theta a_r)}$. Differentiating and simplifying yields

$$\frac{\partial u_r}{\partial i} = \frac{1}{2u_r}\left[\frac{(a_n + \theta a_r)c^2\theta(\theta a_n' + a_r') - [2L\theta + c^2\theta(\theta a_n + a_r)](a_n' + \theta a_r')}{(a_n + \theta a_r)^2} \right]$$

$$\frac{\partial u_n}{\partial i} = \frac{1}{2u_n}\left[\frac{(a_n + \theta a_r)c^2\theta(\theta a_n' + a_r') - [2L\theta + c^2\theta(\theta a_n + a_r)](a_n' + \theta a_r')}{\theta^2(a_n + \theta a_r)^2} \right].$$

Because $u_r > 0$ and $u_n > 0$, it is sufficient to sign the numerators of these two expressions. Expanding the numerator for $\frac{\partial u_r}{\partial i}$ yields $c^2\theta(1 - \theta^2)a_n a_r' + c^2\theta(\theta^2 - 1)a_r a_n' - 2L\theta(a_n' + \theta a_r')$. Multiplying and dividing by $a_n a_r$ and simplifying gives $[c^2\theta(1 - \theta^2)(\varepsilon_r - \varepsilon_n) - 2L\theta(\varepsilon_n / a_r + \theta\varepsilon_r / a_n)]a_n a_r$.

24

Because $1 - \theta^2 < 0$ and $\varepsilon_r < \varepsilon_n < 0$, $\frac{\partial u_r}{\partial i} > 0$. Further, because $u_r = \theta u_n$ and $\theta > 1$, $\frac{\partial u_r}{\partial i} = \theta \frac{\partial u_n}{\partial i} > 0$

so that $\frac{\partial u_r}{\partial i} > \frac{\partial u_n}{\partial i} > 0$. ∎

Proposition 3. *When lenders are capacity constrained and the number of refinance mortgages originated decreases when interest rates rise, a lender's total lending to purchase borrowers could increase when interest rates rise. That is, if $\frac{\partial(u_r-c)a_r}{\partial i} < 0$ then $\frac{\partial(u_n-c)a_n}{\partial i} > 0$ under some conditions. Necessary (but not sufficient) conditions for a rise in interest rates to boost purchase lending include:*

- *$\varepsilon_n \,/\, \varepsilon_r \ll 1$ (where ε_n and ε_r denote the interest rate elasticities of purchase and refinance applications, respectively), i.e., refinance applications are far more interest rate elastic than purchase applications.*

- *$\theta \gg 1$, i.e., purchase applications are more expensive to process and complete than refinance applications.*

<u>Proof.</u> We assume that $\frac{\partial(u_r-c)a_r}{\partial i} = \frac{\partial u_r}{\partial i} a_r + a_r'(u_r - c) < 0$ and are looking for conditions under which

$\frac{\partial(u_n-c)a_n}{\partial i} = \frac{\partial u_n}{\partial i} a_n + a_n'(u_n - c) > 0$. Substituting in u_r, u_n, $\frac{\partial u_r}{\partial i}$, and $\frac{\partial u_n}{\partial i}$ from Proposition 2 and

setting $x \equiv \frac{(a_n+\theta a_r)c^2\theta(\theta a_n'+a_r')-[2L\theta+c^2\theta(\theta a_n+a_r)](a_n'+\theta a_r')}{(a_n+\theta a_r)^2}$ and $u \equiv \left(\frac{2L+c^2(\theta a_n+a_r)}{a_n+\theta a_r}\right)^{\frac{1}{2}}$ gives $\frac{1}{2}\frac{1}{\sqrt{\theta}}u^{-1}x +$

$\varepsilon_r\left(\sqrt{\theta}u - c\right) < 0$ and $\frac{1}{2}\sqrt{\theta}u^{-1}x + \varepsilon_n\left(\frac{1}{\sqrt{\theta}}u - c\right) > 0$. Isolating the $\frac{1}{2}x$ terms gives $\frac{1}{2}x +$

$\sqrt{\theta}u\left(\sqrt{\theta}u - c\right)\varepsilon_r = \frac{1}{2}x + \left(\theta u^2 - \sqrt{\theta}uc\right)\varepsilon_r < 0$ and $\frac{1}{2}x + \frac{1}{\sqrt{\theta}}u\left(\frac{1}{\sqrt{\theta}}u - c\right)\varepsilon_n = \frac{1}{2}x +$

$\left(\frac{1}{\theta}u^2 - \frac{1}{\sqrt{\theta}}uc\right)\varepsilon_n > 0$. For the latter inequality to hold, $|\varepsilon_n|\left(\frac{1}{\theta}u^2 - \frac{1}{\sqrt{\theta}}uc\right) \ll |\varepsilon_r|\left(\theta u^2 - \sqrt{\theta}uc\right)$ so

that $\frac{\varepsilon_n}{\varepsilon_r}\frac{(u-\sqrt{\theta}c)}{\theta(\theta u-\sqrt{\theta}c)} \ll 1$. For this latter inequality to hold, $\varepsilon_n \,/\, \varepsilon_r \ll 1$ and/or $\theta \gg 1$. ∎

25

Photo Rmoved Due to Copyright Restrictions

References

Avery, Robert B., Neil Bhutta, Kenneth P. Brevoort, and Glenn B. Canner (2010b). "The 2009 HMDA Data: The Mortgage Market in a Time of Low Interest Rates and Economic Distress." Federal Reserve Bulletin, 96, A39-77.

Avery, Robert B., Neil Bhutta, Kenneth P. Brevoort, Glenn Canner, and Christa N. Gibbs (2010a). "The 2008 HMDA Data: The Mortgage Market during a Turbulent Year." Federal Reserve Bulletin, 96, A169-211.

Bhutta, Neil (2014). "The Ins and Outs of Mortgage Debt During the Housing Boom and Bust." Unpublished working paper. Board of Governors of the Federal Reserve System.

Bhutta, Neil and Daniel R. Ringo (2014). "The 2013 Home Mortgage Disclosure Act Data." Federal Reserve Bulletin, 100, 1-32.

Campbell, John Y. (2006). "Household Finance." *Journal of Finance*, **61**, 1553-1604.

Demyanyk, Yuliya and Otto van Hemert (2011). "Understanding the Subprime Mortgage Crisis." *Review of Financial Studies*, **24**, 1848-1880.

Deng, Yongheng and John M. Quigley (2006). "Woodhead Behavior and the Pricing of Residential Mortgages." Working Paper Series 1015, Berkeley Program on Housing and Urban Policy.

Fuster, Andreas, Stephanie Lo, and Paul Willen (2014). "Passthrough from the Secondary to the Primary Mortgage Market: From TBA to YSP." Unpublished presentation. Federal Reserve Bank of Boston.

Fuster, Andreas, Laurie Goodman, David Lucca, Laurel Madar, Linsey Molloy, and Paul Willen (2012). "The Rising Gap Between Primary and Secondary Mortgage Rates." Unpublished working paper. Federal Reserve Bank of New York.

Fuster, Andreas and Paul Willen (2010). "$1.25 Trillion is Still Real Money: Some Facts About the Effects of the Federal Reserve's Mortgage Market Investments." FRB Boston Public Policy Discussion Paper Series 10-4.

Hancock, Diana and Wayne Passmore (2014). "Hot the Federal Reserve's Large-Scale Asset Purchases (LSAPs) Influence Mortgage-Backed Securities (MBS) Yields and U.S. Mortgage Rates." Federal Reserve Discussion Series 2004-12.

Mayer, Christopher, Karen Pence, and Shane M. Sherlund (2009). "The Rise in Mortgage Defaults." *Journal of Economic Perspectives*, **23**, 27-50.

Scharfstein, David and Adi Sunderam (2014). "Market Power in Mortgage Lending and the Transmission of Monetary Policy." Unpublished working paper. Harvard University.

Schwartz, Eduardo S. and Walter N. Torous (1989). "Prepayment and the Valuation of Mortgage-Backed Securities." *Journal of Finance*, **44**, 375-392.

Stroebel, Johannes and John B. Taylor (2012). "Estimated Impact of the Federal Reserve's Mortgage-Backed Securities Purchase Program." *International Journal of Central Banking*, **8**, 1-42.

Table 1A: Mortgage Price Sheet

Photo Rmoved Due to Copyright Restrictions

Note: 30-day lock period.

Source: Anonymous lender rate sheet.

Table 1B: Fannie Mae Loan-Level Pricing Adjustments (Percent of Loan Amount)

Photo Rmoved Due to Copyright Restrictions

Loan-level pricing adjustments reported here include 25 basis point adverse-market delivery charge.

Source: Fannie Mae loan-level pricing adjustments as of December 2014.

Table 2: Mortgage Employees

Constant	-2.805***		
	(.683)		
Purchase apps. (t-1)	.196***	Refinance apps. (t-1)	.005
	(.068)		(.022)
Purchase apps. (t-2)	.176***	Refinance apps. (t-2)	.017
	(.065)		(.019)
Purchase apps. (t-3)	.053	Refinance apps. (t-3)	.026
	(.083)		(.018)
Purchase apps. (t-6)	.100	Refinance apps. (t-6)	.014
	(.086)		(.022)
Purchase apps. (t-9)	.015	Refinance apps. (t-9)	.021
	(.082)		(.025)
Purchase apps. (t-12)	-.002	Refinance apps. (t-12)	.026
	(.073)		(.026)
Trend	.001**		
	(.000)		

R-squared: .967

Heteroskedasticity-autocorrelation consistent (HAC) standard errors in parentheses.

*, **, and *** denote statistical significance at the 90%, 95%, and 99% confidence levels.

Dependent variable: log(Mortgage employees): $\log(L)_t$.

Sample period: January 2003 – September 2014.

Data sources: Mortgage employees from Bureau of Labor Statistics (BLS); mortgage
   applications from Home Mortgage Disclosure Act (HMDA) data.

Table 3: Credit Scores on Prime GSE Purchase Originations (Primary Specification)

July 2009 – Sep. 2014	Purchase Originations	Refinance Originations	Purchase-Refinance
Constant	699.56***	676.76***	22.79***
	(.26)	(1.20)	(1.34)
$(a_r/L)_{t-1}$	1.48***	4.07***	-2.59*
	(.32)	(1.22)	(1.43)
Trend	-.04	-.07	.02
	(.06)	(.31)	(.36)
Δ House prices	10.36	-112.48***	122.84***
	(7.71)	(41.09)	(44.30)
Δ Mtg rates	-.06	.26	-.33
	(.78)	(3.50)	(3.96)
Unemp rate	2.76***	2.98	-.22
	(.85)	(3.85)	(4.38)
R-squared	.933	.879	.748

Jan. 2003 – June 2007	Purchase Originations	Refinance Originations	Purchase-Refinance
Constant	644.78***	638.15***	6.63***
	(.41)	(.41)	(.55)
$(a_r/L)_{t-1}$	1.53***	2.87***	-1.34***
	(.32)	(.40)	(.49)
Trend	.10	-.21**	.31*
	(.12)	(.10)	(.18)
Δ House prices	62.91***	13.41*	49.50***
	(11.58)	(7.22)	(12.99)
Δ Mtg rates	1.10	-3.34***	4.44***
	(1.13)	(.76)	(1.01)
Unemp. rate	-1.19	-7.48***	6.29
	(3.23)	(2.74)	(4.81)
R-squared	.745	.903	.827

Heteroskedasticity-autocorrelation consistent (HAC) standard errors in parentheses.

*, **, and *** denote statistical significance at the 90%, 95%, and 99% confidence levels.

Dependent variable: 10th-percentile credit score: $(1 - u)_t$.

Sample periods: January 2003 – June 2007 and July 2009 – September 2014.

Data sources: 10th-percentile credit scores calculated from LPS / Black Knight data; applications per mortgage employee calculated from Home Mortgage Disclosure Act (HMDA) and Bureau of Labor Statistics (BLS) data; house prices changes calculated from CoreLogic data; mortgage rates calculated from Freddie Mac and Optimal Blue (formerly LoanSifter) data; unemployment rate from the Bureau of Labor Statistics (BLS).

Table 4: Prime GSE Purchase Originations (Primary Specification)

July 2009 – Sep. 2014		Credit Score					
	<=620	621-680	681-710	711-740	741-770	771-790	>790
Constant	8.628	-3.550**	-5.866**	-6.867**	-8.268***	-6.550**	-3.909*
	(7.400)	(1.550)	(2.694)	(2.853)	(2.944)	(2.491)	(1.973)
$(a_r/L)_{t-1}$	-.079*	-.063***	-.030**	-.015	.002	.014	.022***
	(.042)	(.009)	(.012)	(.011)	(.010)	(.009)	(.007)
$log(a_n)_{t-1}$	2.638***	.906***	1.078***	1.210***	1.273***	1.073***	.865***
	(.552)	(.098)	(.153)	(.156)	(.164)	(.143)	(.118)
Trend	-.110***	.007***	.008**	.007*	.009**	.010***	.011***
	(.011)	(.002)	(.003)	(.004)	(.004)	(.003)	(.002)
Unemp rate	-1.540***	-.118***	-.067	-.056	.002	.057	.064*
	(.169)	(.039)	(.053)	(.063)	(.057)	(.047)	(.036)
R-squared	.712	.948	.909	.865	.844	.811	.812

Jan. 2003 – June 2007		Credit Score					
	<=620	621-680	681-710	711-740	741-770	771-790	>790
Constant	14.247***	5.640***	2.450***	1.739*	1.119	-.921	-6.140**
	(1.899)	(.881)	(.728)	(.903)	(.827)	(.913)	(2.293)
$(a_r/L)_{t-1}$	-.001	-.017***	-.004	-.002	-.006	-.002	.023**
	(.013)	(.005)	(.004)	(.004)	(.004)	(.005)	(.010)
$log(a_n)_{t-1}$	-.332***	.381***	.640***	.724***	.793***	.956***	1.331***
	(.106)	(.071)	(.050)	(.061)	(.054)	(.071)	(.136)
Trend	-.001	-.002	-.003**	-.005***	-.007***	-.008***	-.002
	(.003)	(.001)	(.001)	(.001)	(.001)	(.002)	(.004)
Unemp. rate	-.039	.068	.003	-.001	.037	-.029	-.253**
	(.089)	(.044)	(.040)	(.045)	(.050)	(.059)	(.108)
R-squared	.314	.667	.788	.808	.872	.854	.874

Heteroskedasticity-autocorrelation consistent (HAC) standard errors in parentheses.

*, **, and *** denote statistical significance at the 90%, 95%, and 99% confidence levels.

Dependent variable: log(purchase mortgage originations) by credit-score group: $log(u_n a_n)_{it}$.

Sample periods: January 2003 – June 2007 and July 2009 – September 2014.

Data sources: Mortgage originations calculated from LPS / Black Knight and Home Mortgage Disclosure Act (HMDA) data; applications per mortgage employee calculated from Home Mortgage Disclosure Act (HMDA) and Bureau of Labor Statistics (BLS) data; mortgage applications from Home Mortgage Disclosure Act (HMDA) data; unemployment rate from the Bureau of Labor Statistics (BLS).

Table 5: Credit Scores on Prime GSE Purchase Originations (Nonlinear Capacity Effect)

July 2009 – Sep. 2014	Purchase Originations	Refinance Originations	Purchase-Refinance
Constant	699.56***	676.76***	22.79***
	(.31)	(1.21)	(1.32)
$\max\left\{\left(\frac{a_r}{L}\right)_{t-1} - \frac{\overline{a_r}}{L}, 0\right\}$	1.59**	6.16***	-4.57***
	(.68)	(1.47)	(1.59)
Trend	.05	.10	-.05
	(.07)	(.34)	(.36)
Δ House prices	20.62**	-87.86**	108.47**
	(8.52)	(43.54)	(45.25)
Δ Mtg rates	-2.03**	-3.81	1.78
	(.79)	(2.47)	(2.63)
Unemp rate	4.82***	7.35*	-2.53
	(1.02)	(4.03)	(4.38)
R-squared	.898	.869	.749

Jan. 2003 – June 2007	Purchase Originations	Refinance Originations	Purchase-Refinance
Constant	644.78***	638.15***	6.63***
	(.43)	(.42)	(.55)
$\max\left\{\left(\frac{a_r}{L}\right)_{t-1} - \frac{\overline{a_r}}{L}, 0\right\}$	1.46***	2.83***	-1.38***
	(.33)	(.41)	(.49)
Trend	.11	-.20**	.31*
	(.12)	(.10)	(.18)
Δ House prices	65.80***	19.79**	46.01***
	(12.21)	(7.86)	(13.01)
Δ Mtg rates	.84	-3.72***	4.56***
	(1.16)	(.71)	(.97)
Unemp. rate	-.63	-6.58**	5.95*
	(3.24)	(2.58)	(4.70)
R-squared	.732	.901	.830

Heteroskedasticity-autocorrelation consistent (HAC) standard errors in parentheses.

*, **, and *** denote statistical significance at the 90%, 95%, and 99% confidence levels.

Dependent variable: 10th-percentile credit score: $(1 - u)_t$.

Sample periods: January 2003 – June 2007 and July 2009 – September 2014.

Data sources: 10th-percentile credit scores calculated from LPS / Black Knight data; applications per mortgage employee calculated from Home Mortgage Disclosure Act (HMDA) and Bureau of Labor Statistics (BLS) data; house prices changes calculated from CoreLogic data; mortgage rates calculated from Freddie Mac and Optimal Blue (formerly LoanSifter) data; unemployment rate from the Bureau of Labor Statistics (BLS).

Table 6: Prime GSE Purchase Originations (Nonlinear Capacity Effect)

July 2009 –	Credit Score						
Sep. 2014	<=620	621-680	681-710	711-740	741-770	771-790	>790
Constant	12.735*	-.336	-4.393**	-6.177***	-8.505***	-7.404***	-5.180**
	(6.647)	(1.239)	(1.994)	(2.313)	(2.707)	(2.565)	(2.299)
$\max\left\{\left(\frac{a_r}{L}\right)_{t-1} - \frac{\overline{a_r}}{L}, 0\right\}$	-.167*	-.138***	-.072***	-.042**	-.015	.010	.027*
	(.096)	(.017)	(.022)	(.020)	(.016)	(.014)	(.014)
$log(a_n)_{t-1}$	2.365***	.686***	.970***	1.153***	1.268***	1.109***	.929***
	(.535)	(.083)	(.120)	(.133)	(.157)	(.154)	(.143)
Trend	-.112***	.006***	.008***	.007*	.010***	.012***	.012***
	(.010)	(.002)	(.003)	(.004)	(.003)	(.003)	(.002)
Unemp rate	-1.600***	-.162***	-.083**	-.060	.016	.081*	.094**
	(.146)	(.031)	(.041)	(.054)	(.053)	(.048)	(.040)
R-squared	.711	.949	.914	.870	.846	.801	.790

Jan. 2003 –	Credit Score						
June 2007	<=620	621-680	681-710	711-740	741-770	771-790	>790
Constant	14.205***	5.751***	2.487***	1.773	1.174	-.840	-6.078**
	(1.905)	(.856)	(.725)	(.905)	(.815)	(.893)	(2.319)
$\max\left\{\left(\frac{a_r}{L}\right)_{t-1} - \frac{\overline{a_r}}{L}, 0\right\}$	.000	-.018***	-.005	-.003	-.007	-.004	.020*
	(.012)	(.005)	(.004)	(.004)	(.004)	(.004)	(.010)
$log(a_n)_{t-1}$	-.329***	.366***	.636***	.721***	.786***	.949***	1.334***
	(.110)	(.069)	(.051)	(.062)	(.053)	(.071)	(.140)
Trend	-.001	-.002	-.003**	-.005***	-.007***	-.008***	-.002
	(.003)	(.001)	(.001)	(.001)	(.001)	(.002)	(.004)
Unemp. rate	-.040	.066	.003	.000	.037	-.027	-.244**
	(.089)	(.044)	(.040)	(.044)	(.049)	(.058)	(.109)
R-squared	.314	.677	.789	.808	.873	.855	.871

Heteroskedasticity-autocorrelation consistent (HAC) standard errors in parentheses.

*, **, and *** denote statistical significance at the 90%, 95%, and 99% confidence levels.

Dependent variable: log(purchase mortgage originations) by credit-score group: $log(u_n a_n)_{it}$.

Sample periods: January 2003 – June 2007 and July 2009 – September 2014.

Data sources: Mortgage originations calculated from LPS / Black Knight and Home Mortgage Disclosure Act (HMDA) data; applications per mortgage employee calculated from Home Mortgage Disclosure Act (HMDA) and Bureau of Labor Statistics (BLS) data; mortgage applications from Home Mortgage Disclosure Act (HMDA) data; unemployment rate from the Bureau of Labor Statistics (BLS).

Table 7: Credit Scores on Prime GSE Purchase Originations (Price Measure of Capacity Utilization)

Photo Rmoved Due to Copyright Restrictions

Heteroskedasticity-autocorrelation consistent (HAC) standard errors in parentheses.

*, **, and *** denote statistical significance at the 90%, 95%, and 99% confidence levels.

Dependent variable: 10th-percentile credit score: $(1 - u)_t$.

Sample periods: January 2003 – June 2007 and July 2009 – September 2014.

Data sources: 10th-percentile credit scores calculated from LPS / Black Knight data; mortgage-rate spread calculated from Freddie Mac, Optimal Blue (formerly LoanSifter) and Barclays data; house prices changes calculated from CoreLogic data; mortgage rates calculated from Freddie Mac and Optimal Blue (formerly LoanSifter) data; unemployment rate from the Bureau of Labor Statistics (BLS).

Figure 2A: GSE Purchase Originations by Credit Score (Low Credit Scores)

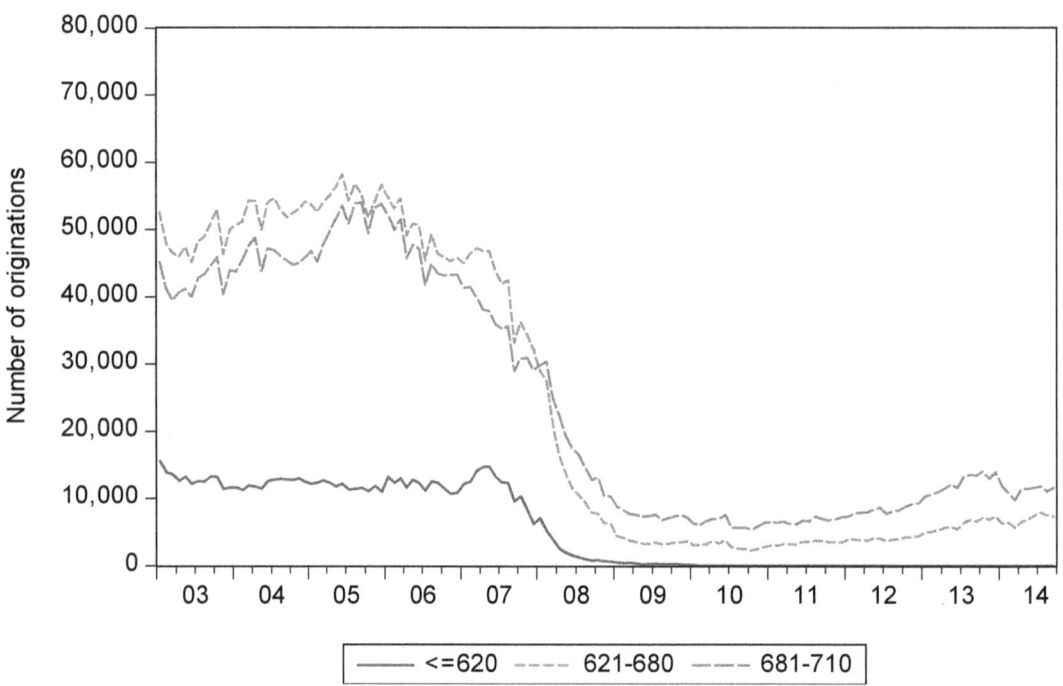

Figure 2B: GSE Purchase Originations by Credit Score (High Credit Scores)

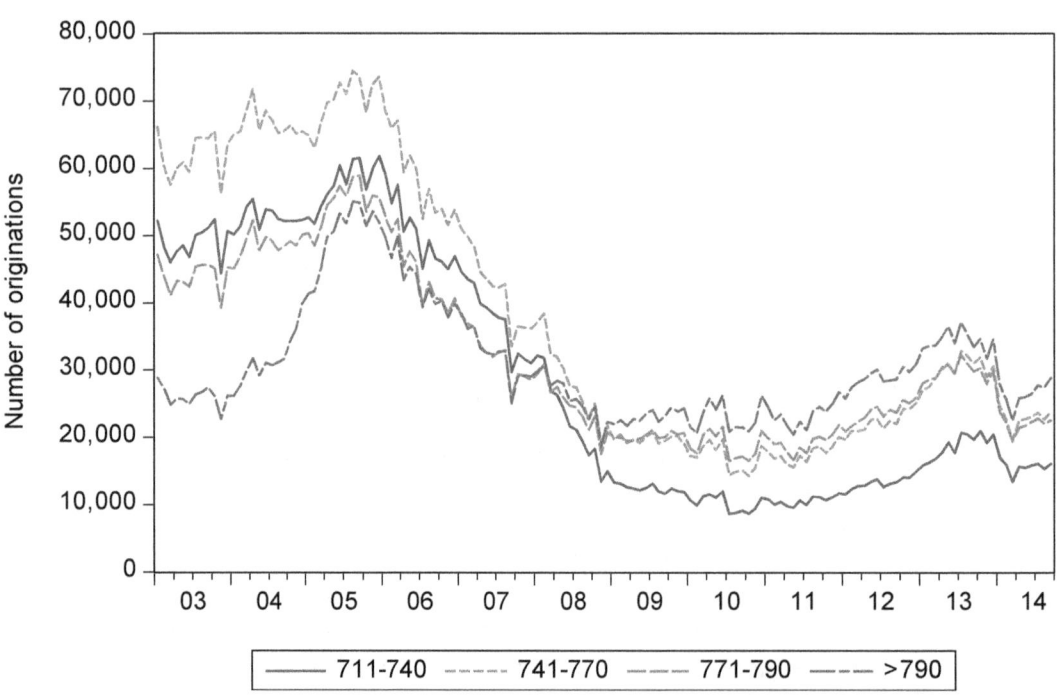

Source: Authors' estimates from Home Mortgage Disclosure Act (HMDA) and LPS / Black Knight data.

Figure 4A: Refinance Applications vs Mortgage-Related Employees

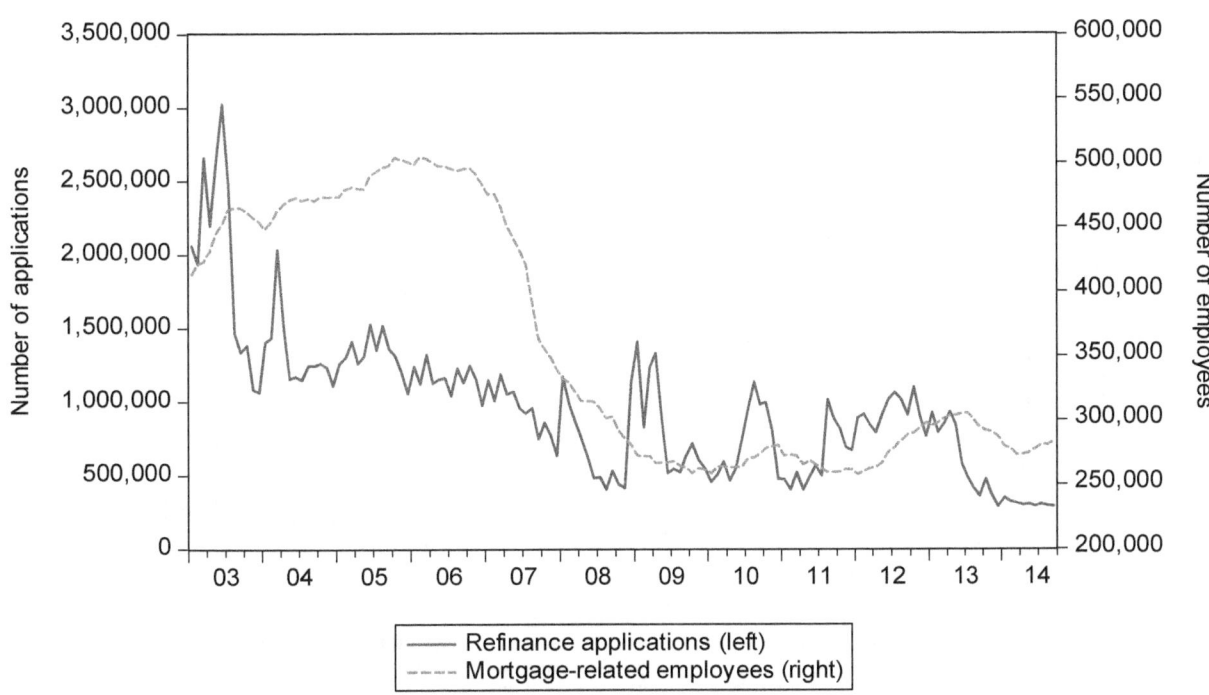

Refinance applications (left)
Mortgage-related employees (right)

Figure 4B: Capacity Utilization

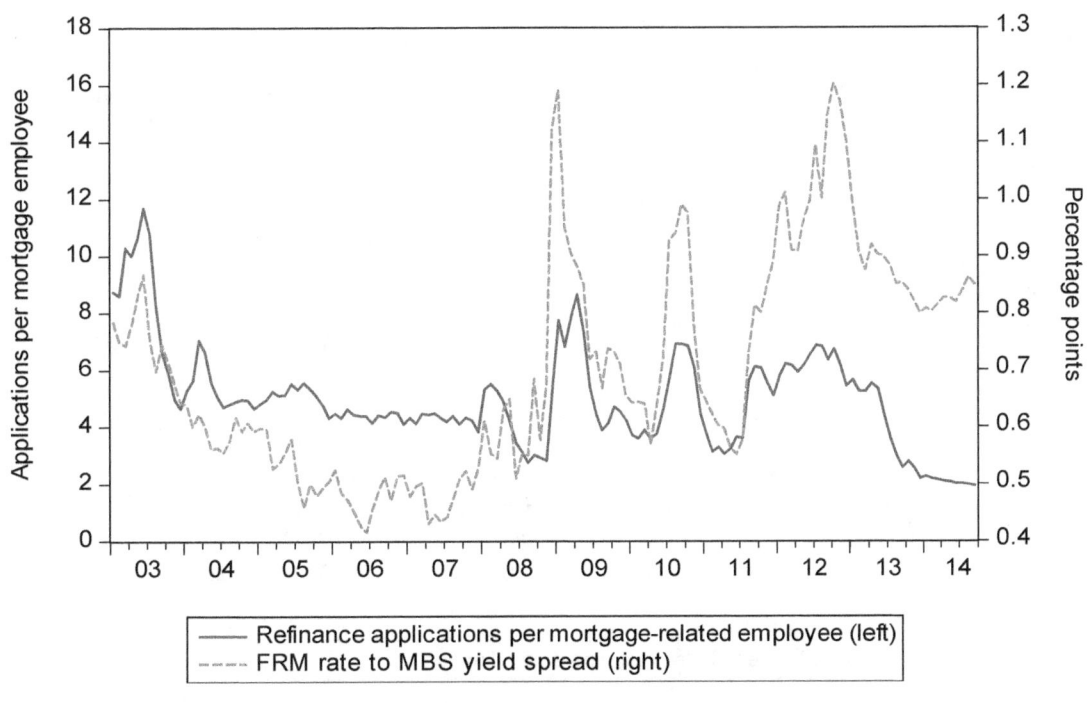

Refinance applications per mortgage-related employee (left)
FRM rate to MBS yield spread (right)

Source: For mortgage employees, Bureau of Labor Statistics (BLS); for refinance applications, Home Mortgage Disclosure Act (HMDA) data; for fixed-rate mortgage rate, Freddie Mac and Optimal Blue (formerly LoanSifter) data; for MBS yield, Barclays.

Figure 5A: 10ᵗʰ-Percentile Credit Scores on Purchase Originations vs Capacity Utilization

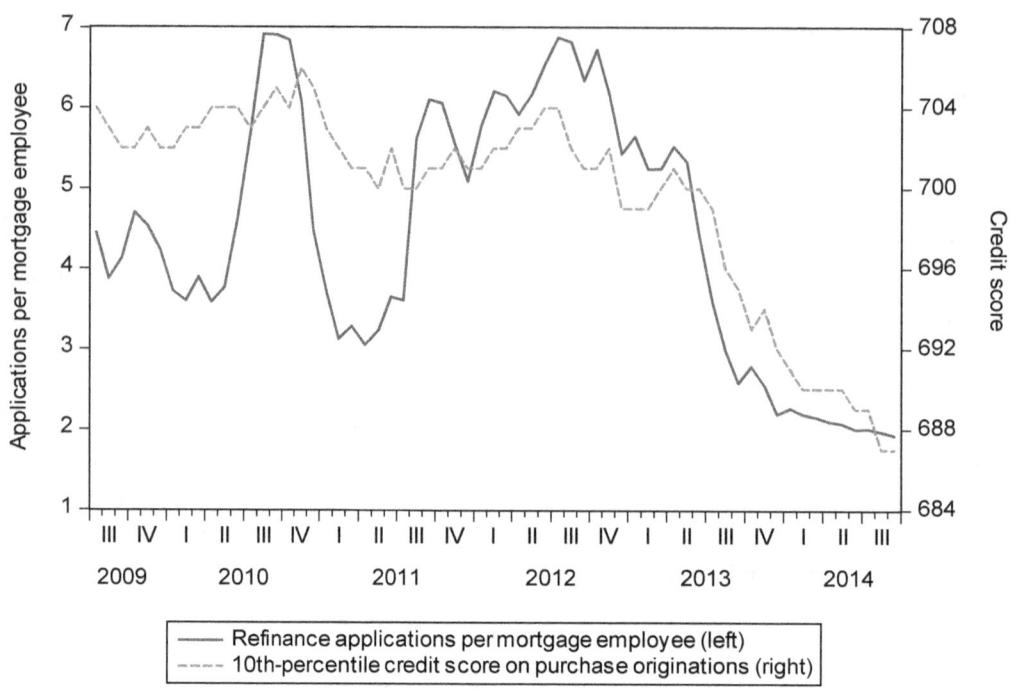

Figure 5B: 10ᵗʰ-Percentile Credit Scores on Refinance Originations vs Capacity Utilization

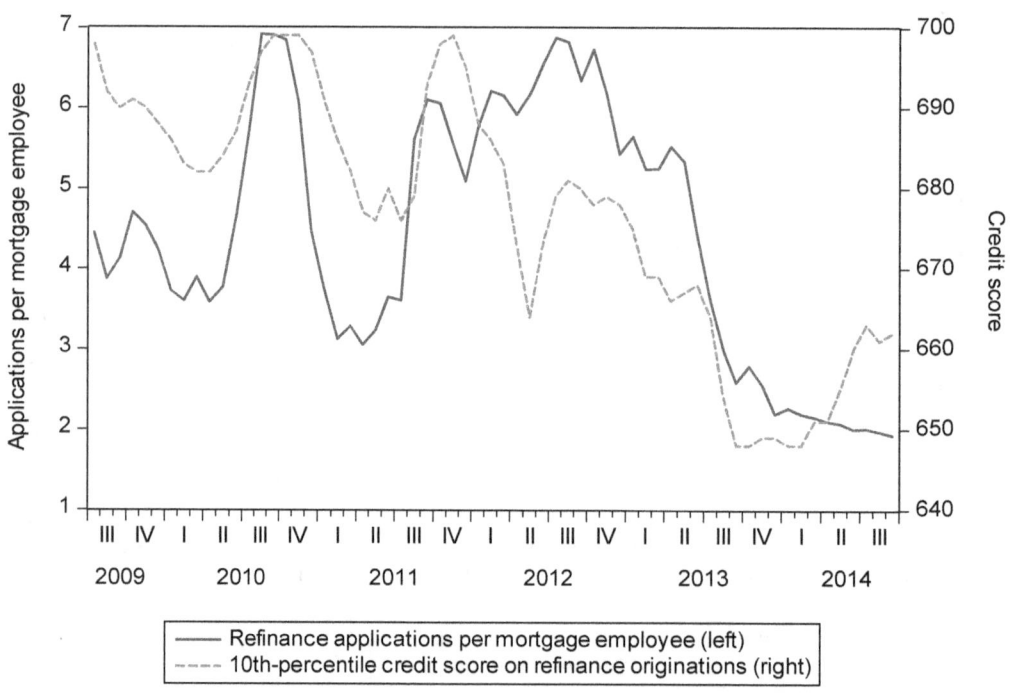

Source: For mortgage employees, Bureau of Labor Statistics (BLS); for refinance applications, Home Mortgage Disclosure Act (HMDA) data; for 10ᵗʰ-percentile credit scores, LPS / Black Knight data.

Figure 6A: Purchase Applications by Credit Score (Low Credit Scores)

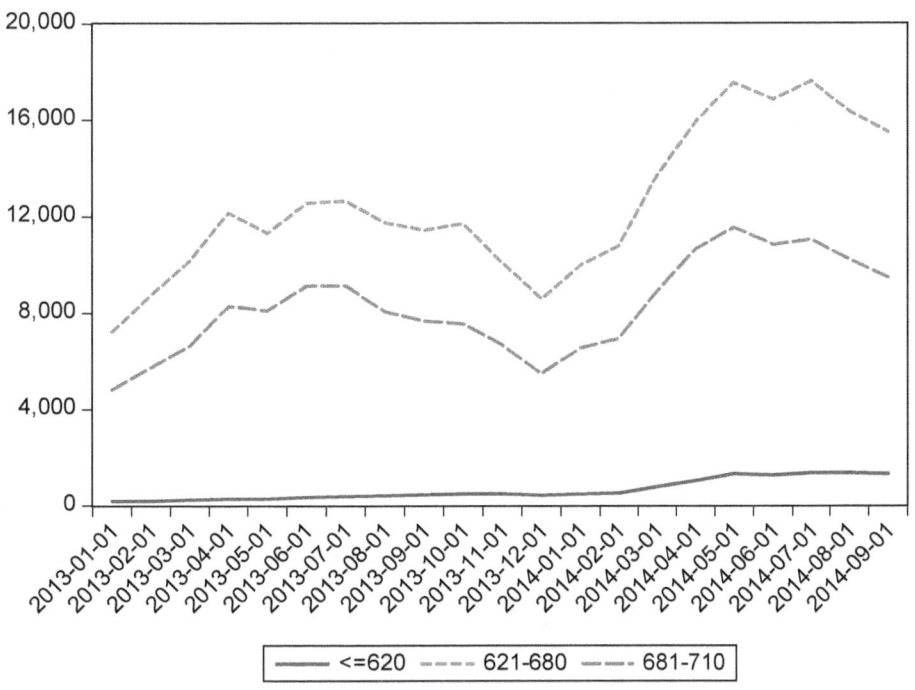

Figure 6B: Purchase Applications by Credit Score (High Credit Scores)

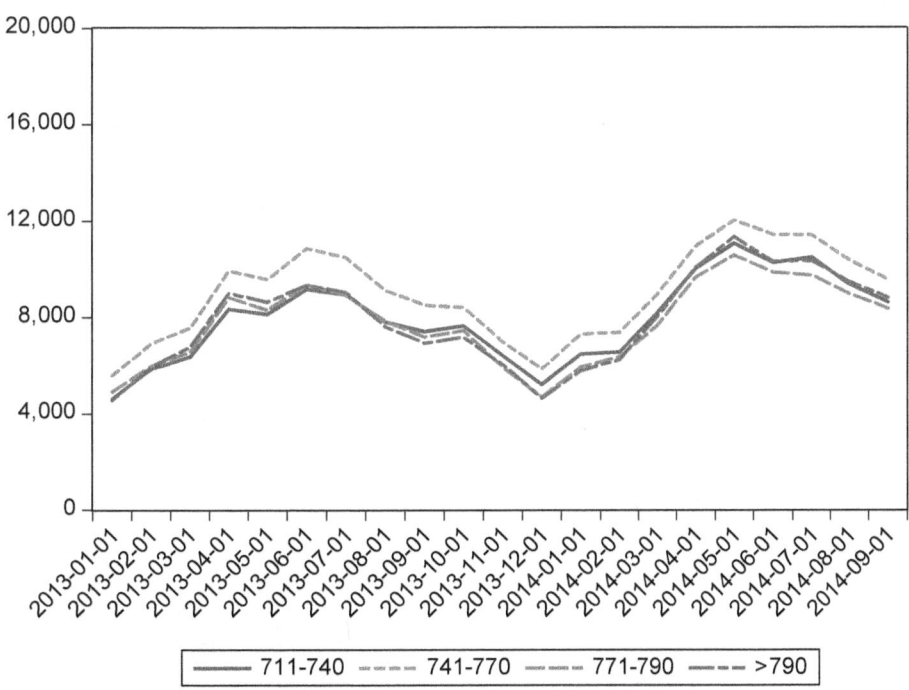

Source: Estimates based on Optimal Blue data, and does not contain lender or customer identities.

www.ingramcontent.com/pod-product-compliance
Lightning Source LLC
Chambersburg PA
CBHW080621180526

45168CB00007B/3006